Review Copy
Not For Sale

The Evolution of
Government &
Politics

The Evolution of
Government and
Politics in
CHINA

CHINA

Great Hall of the People,
Beijing, China

Earle Rice Jr.

Mitchell Lane
PUBLISHERS
P.O. Box 196
Hockessin, DE 19707

BUTLER MIDDLE SCHOOL
MEDIA CENTER
310 NORTH HINE AVENUE
WAUKESHA, WI 53188

Mitchell Lane
PUBLISHERS

The Evolution of Government &
Politics

The Evolution of Government and Politics in

CHINA
EGYPT
FRANCE
GERMANY
GREECE
IRAQ
ITALY
NORTH AND SOUTH KOREA
THE UNITED KINGDOM
VENEZUELA

Copyright © 2015 by Mitchell Lane
Publishers

All rights reserved. No part of this book may
be reproduced without written permission
from the publisher. Printed and bound in
the United States of America.

PUBLISHER'S NOTE: The facts in this book
have been thoroughly researched.
Documentation of such research can be
found on pages 44–45. While every possible
effort has been made to ensure accuracy, the
publisher will not assume liability for
damages caused by inaccuracies in the data,
and makes no warranty on the accuracy of
the information contained herein.
The Internet sites referenced herein were
active as of the publication date. Due to the
fleeting nature of some web sites, we cannot
guarantee that they will all be active when
you are reading this book.

Printing   1   2   3   4   5   6   7   8   9

Library of Congress
Cataloging-in-Publication Data

Rice, Earle.
 The evolution of government and politics in
China / by Earle Rice Jr.
    pages. cm. — (The evolution of
government and politics)
 Includes bibliographical references and
index.
 ISBN 978-1-61228-581-8 (library bound)
1. China—Politics and government—Juvenile
literature. I. Title.
JQ1510.R54 2015
320.951—dc23
                                                        2014008836

eBook ISBN: 9781612286181

PBP

Contents

CHAPTER 1

Looking Back to See the Future

The suspension bridge at Luding, China, stretched 360 feet (110 meters) across the Dadu River's swirling current. Irregularly laid planking formed crude flooring for the open-sided, single span of 13 iron chains. Soldiers loyal to Chinese Nationalist leader Chiang Kai-shek had removed most of the wooden floor planks. The bare chains swung free and swayed precariously. A gatehouse, set in a 20-foot-high (6 meters) stone wall on the east bank of the river, commanded the approaches. The wall bristled with machine guns.

Yang Chenwu's Red Army regiment arrived at Luding on the west bank of the river at daybreak on May 29, 1935. Chiang's soldiers were preparing to set fire to the bridge's remaining floor planks. In something of an understatement, Yang later said, "We were taken aback at the difficulties to be overcome."[1]

But the difficulties had to be overcome. The main body of Chiang's army was in hot pursuit and heavily outnumbered Yang's forces. Yang quickly

Pedestrians stroll across the Luding Bridge. It is constructed of iron chains and wooden planking lashed over the chains to form a roadway. The bridge was the site of an important incident during the Long March in 1935.

surveyed the situation and called for volunteers. Twenty-two men stepped forward. Strapping hand grenades and German-made Mauser rifles to their backs, they inched out onto the bridge and crawled crablike along the chains on each side. Yang's machine gunners laid down supporting fire. Chiang's gunners returned fire, and snipers began picking off the Reds working their way toward them on the swaying bridge. The lead volunteer was hit and dropped into the roiling waters below. Then a second man fell. And a third. But on they crawled, those volunteers.

These men were warriors, the likes of whom which the peasants of Sichuan province had likely never seen before. Amid the whiz and clatter of machine-gun bullets, one man finally reached the bridge's remaining planking and crawled up onto it. Ignoring the heavy fire, he uncapped a grenade, raised up, and threw a perfect strike into the enemy position. Chiang's soldiers responded, tossing kerosene onto the planking and setting it aflame.

Other Reds reached the planking. They doused the fire and replaced the boards. Eighteen of the 22 volunteers reached the east bank of the Dadu, while Chiang's aircraft buzzed angrily overhead but were powerless to stop their advance. Within two hours, Yang Chenwu's forces had overrun the Nationalist garrison and captured the town of Luding.

A few days later, the entire army of communist leader Mao Zedong reached the bridge and crossed the Dadu safely. Because of the heroics of 22 volunteers, Mao and his ragtag forces would live to fight another day.

Or so the story was reported for about a half-century. Recently, however, a biography of Mao by Jung Chang and Jon Halliday casts doubt on this legendary saga.

Chang and Halliday contend that the whole tale is fiction, and that "there was no battle at the Dadu Bridge."[2] They go on to portray a more likely scenario in which there was a skirmish but not a battle. Nor were there any crab-crawling heroics. When the main body of the Red Army reached the river, Chang and Halliday further assert, the garrison commander at the bridge telephoned his superiors for instructions. He indicated it would be difficult to hold out against Mao's superior forces. When the phone line went dead, he panicked and ordered a retreat.

This updated version of the Dadu Bridge incident lacks the drama and raw courage of the tale's original telling. In both accounts, however, the endings coincide: Chiang Kai-shek's Nationalist Army failed to contain—and destroy—Mao Zedong's Red Army. What came to be known as the Long March continued. And China moved farther down its long path toward communism.

A young Mao Zedong delivers an inspiring speech to a crowd of his followers during the Long March of 1934–35. Many historians cite the Long March as perhaps the greatest military march of all time.

Long ago, the venerated Chinese philosopher Confucius said, "Study the past if you would divine the future."[3] With respect to his homeland, it means that one must study China's long history to understand modern China and how it became what it is today.

For most of this history, hereditary monarchies known as dynasties ruled China. They began with the legendary—or mythical—Xia (Hsia) dynasty (c.2205–c.1766 BCE). The Shang dynasty (c.1600–1046 BCE) followed the Xia. It introduced a writing system and began recording Chinese history for the first time. China's longest-lasting dynasty, the Zhou (1046–256 BCE), defeated the Shangs at the Battle of Muye and assumed control.

China is one of the world's oldest civilizations. Thriving cultures existed in the Huang (Yellow) River Valley as early as 3000 BCE.

King Wu of the Zhou dynasty

But its final centuries were characterized by a breakup into a number of smaller states that were often at war with each other.

Even though the Qin dynasty (221–206 BCE) lasted only a few years, its founders conquered several states and formed the first great Chinese empire. It established the approximate boundaries and basic administrative system that all subsequent dynasties would follow. Its many accomplishments included the standardization of the Chinese writing system and the construction of the Great Wall of China.

For more than 2,000 years, succeeding dynasties ruled China. The vast country expanded, broke apart, and put itself back together during its stormy history. A long chain of emperors presided over all manner of catastrophic events: invasions, foreign rule, civil wars and rebellions, and all kinds of natural disasters. Chinese subjects assigned near-divine status and a Mandate from Heaven to their emperors. But an emperor without an empire is like a captain without a ship.

"Emperors might be quasi-divine," writes author and journalist Jonathan Fenby, "but it was not assumed that dynasties were for ever. . . . When the gods showed their displeasure, for instance by permitting major revolts or visiting particularly severe natural disasters upon the country, it was time for a change."[4]

The last dynastic change in China occurred in 1644. An army of peasants led by Li Tzu-ch'eng breached the Great Wall and captured the Chinese capital at Beijing (then known as Peking). Desperate officials of the Ming dynasty—which dated back to 1368—called on the Manchus for help.

In 1636, the Manchus had established the Qing (Ch'ing) dynasty in their native Manchuria, a region northeast of China. Taking advantage of the Mings' urgent situation, the Manchus seized Beijing and established their own dynasty in the Chinese capital. In the following decades, they conquered the rest of China at the cost of an estimated 25 million lives. Under the

Great Wall of China

China, measured by its landmass of 3,696,853 square miles (9,569,901 square kilometers), is the second-largest country in the world. Only Russia is larger.

Guangxu (Kuang-hsu) Emperor (1871–1908) was the 11th Qing emperor. He reigned from 1875 to 1908. In practice, however, his rule was heavily influenced by the Empress Dowager Cixi.

Manchus, China expanded its territory into Central Asia and increased its population from about 100 million to nearly 400 million.

In the early 1800s, problems over increased population and land ownership began to trouble Qing bureaucrats. While Manchu armies deteriorated, civil unrest began to rise, aggravated by severe floods and famine. A series of popular revolts erupted, most notably the Taiping Rebellion (1850–64) and the Nien Rebellion (1851–68). The Opium Wars with Great Britain (and later France) between 1839 and 1858 further weakened the Qing regime. During this time of rebellions and wars, untold millions of Chinese lost their lives.

At the start of the twentieth century, the rule of the Qing dynasty grew steadily weaker. And one last rebellion would hasten its demise.

A scene from the Nien Rebellion (1851–1868) that probably portrays the Battle of Inlon River (1867). The rebellion caused enormous economic devastation and loss of life and greatly contributed to the eventual collapse of the Qing regime in the early 20th century.

CHAPTER 2
Two Leaders Emerge

The turbulence sweeping across China in the latter part of the nineteenth century was reflected in its rulers. A low-ranking concubine (mistress) of Emperor Xianfeng named Cixi (Tz'u-his) bore his only son, Tongzhi. Tongzhi became emperor at the age of six upon his father's death in 1861 and Cixi became Dowager Empress. In effect, she controlled the dynasty and wielded the real power. When Tongzhi died in 1875, Cixi named her adoptive nephew, three-year-old Guangxu, to succeed him. She remained the power behind the throne.

Though Cixi put down rebellions, China suffered a major defeat in the Sino-Japanese War of 1894–1895. At the turn of the century, China was bankrupt from the war and taxes were rising. Penetrations by foreign powers deep into China had left its economy in shambles. Popular discontent and resistance to foreign intrusion were growing. Enter the Boxers, a secret society opposed to foreigners.

The powerful and charismatic Empress Dowager Cixi is depicted here at about age 55. Cixi unofficially but effectively controlled the Manchu Qing dynasty for 47 years, from 1861 to her death in 1908.

The Boxers practiced Chinese Boxing, or *Wushu*, hence the name used by most foreigners. They also performed calisthenic rituals, which they believed gave them supernatural powers and made them impervious to bullets. The Boxers called themselves *Yihequan*—the Fists of Righteousness and Harmony.

In 1900, the Boxers began attacking foreigners all over northern China. "Entire Christian families, including children, were hacked to death with swords," writes journalist Bertil Lintner. "Churches and railway stations were burned, factories ransacked and telegraph lines cut. Then the Fists marched on Beijing."[1] That began a 55-day siege of the city's foreign legation quarter.

Britain, France, Germany, Japan, Austria, Russia, Italy, and the United States sent troops to suppress the Boxers and lift the siege. The eight-nation force put down the rebellion and demanded huge reparations. Approximately 115,000 people died in the Boxer Rebellion. And civil unrest continued to fester.

Emperor Guangxu died on November 14, 1908. Some say that Cixi ordered Guangxu poisoned. She died the following day, just after naming the grandson of her former lover as the next emperor. At the age of two years and 10 months, the new ruler was given the reign name of Puyi. He became the last emperor of China. Guangxu's consort, Longyu, assumed the title of Empress Dowager.

In October 1911, a rebellion against the Qing dynasty broke out in Wuchang in central China. Rebels waved white flags edged

British and Japanese forces engage the Boxers in a battle at the machine works in T'ien-chin, China. The uprising, between 1898 and 1900, was a violent anti-foreign and anti-Christian movement that attempted to oust foreign elements from China. An eight-nation alliance intervened and defeated Chinese forces.

The Boxers originated in the early eighteenth century as a secret society. They tried—but failed—to overthrow the Qing (Manchu) dynasty and restore the Ming dynasty. The Boxers were put down, but the superstition of magical boxing kept the sect alive in the shadows until its revival in 1898.

with red, bearing the legend: *Xin Han, Mie Man*—"Long live the Han, Exterminate the Manchu."[2] The Han Chinese constitute roughly 92 percent of China's population, and felt they should be in control. And the slaughter of Manchus began.

The revolt spread quickly through the central and southern regions of the country. Inspired by the republican movement of Dr. Sun Yat-sen, it became known as the Xinhai (or Chinese) Revolution. It claimed tens of thousands of casualties and about two thousand fatalities.

The revolution ended with the establishment of the Republic of China on January 1, 1912. Six-year-old Emperor Puyi abdicated a month later. After more than 2,000 years of imperial rule, China's monarchy had given way to a new republic with democratic principles. Sun Yat-sen, leader of the Chinese Nationalist Party, or Guomindang (GMD), emerged as the provisional president of the new republic.

On March 10, 1912, the National Assembly in Nanjing elected former army general Yuan Shikai as president. Sun Yat-sen stepped down. In a farewell speech, he vowed, "It will be my object to help my 400,000,000 countrymen, and to endeavour to make the blessings of the Republic a reality."[3] As Yuan's future actions revealed, he held less noble aspirations than Sun Yat-sen.

On December 23, 1915, Yuan Shikai shed his military uniform and donned a traditional robe of purple with circular dragons. On the altar of the Temple of Heaven in Beijing's Forbidden City, he declared himself emperor. He took the reign name of Hongxian ("Constitutional Abundance"). His claims to the Mandate of

Heaven did not last long. Public outrage forced his abdication on March 21, 1916 and he died of blood poisoning later that summer.

Though the world continued to recognize the Beijing-based government, it soon became virtually powerless. Regional warlords controlled most of Chinese territory and held the real power in the fragmented nation. "Beijing is like a crucible," wrote Mao Zedong, "in which one cannot but be transformed."[4] Mao was then a young student who had joined the army to fight in the revolution, but he had seen no action. After six months of garrison duty in Changsha, Mao resigned from the army and returned to his studies. He would play a far larger role in China's future in the years to come.

In the autumn of 1920, Mao helped to found a Marxist study circle in Changsha and a radical bookstore specializing in communist tracts. Soon afterward, he declared himself a communist to his colleagues. In July 1921, thirteen delegates from China's various communist groups met secretly in Shanghai. They convened the First Congress of the Chinese Communist

Yuan Shikai (center, with hat removed) was a Chinese general, politician, and emperor. Yuan wielded great influence during the last days of the Qing dynasty. He was known for his autocratic rule as the first president of the Republic of China (1912–16) and his unsuccessful attempt to restore the monarchy in China with himself as emperor.

The Xinhai Revolution was named for the Chinese year of Xinhai (1911). It began with the Wuchang Uprising, a mutiny of army units stationed in the city of Wuchang.

Party (CCP). The scholarly Mao immersed himself in the cause that would consume the rest of his life.

Meanwhile, Sun Yat-sen sought asylum in Japan after leading an unsuccessful revolt against Yuan Shikai. He returned to China with dreams of reuniting his fragmented nation. Chiang Kai-shek joined him as his chief military aide. Sun died in 1925 before realizing his dreams. Chiang rose to prominence in the GMD as the leader of the National Revolutionary Army. The GMD and the CCP formed an alliance called the United Front to take back China from the warlords.

Chiang led a series of nimble military and political maneuvers known collectively as the Northern Expedition (1926–27) to defeat the warlords. He established Nanjing as the capital of his right-wing, civilian-military regime. Chiang then turned on his former CCP allies. First he expelled them from Nanjing. Then in April 1927, he arrested many communists in Shanghai. He executed at least 300 and many more went missing. Soon afterward, the forces of the GMD and the CCP began a civil war that would last, intermittently, for the next 22 years.

Mao Zedong was by then an emerging communist leader. In August, he mounted a peasant offensive against the Nationalists called the Autumn Harvest Uprising. It failed miserably, but Mao learned a valuable lesson. "From now on, we must pay the greatest attention to military affairs," he told his fellow communists. "We must know that political power is obtained from the barrel of a gun."[5]

In May 1928, Mao merged his forces with those of Zhu De, another communist military leader. Together, they created the 8,000-man Fourth Red Army (or the Mao-Zhu Army). Significantly, red is the color of international communism. Mao's fight with Nationalist leader Chiang Kai-shek was underway.

CHAPTER 3
Fighting for China's Future

In January 1928, Chiang Kai-shek was named Generalissimo of all Chinese forces and chairman of the National Government. Chiang's government was essentially a one-party dictatorship. His capture of Beijing in June that year supposedly unified China. In reality, warlords still controlled many areas. And the growing communist movement forced him to conduct five Encirclement Campaigns (1930–34) against them in southern China, where the communists had established a number of rural bases.

The CCP fought off the first four, but Chiang mustered about 700,000 troops for the fifth and final one, which began in September 1933. A year later, Chiang's armies forced the remnants of the Red Army to evacuate their base in Jiangxi province. The army was then under the joint leadership of Soviet-schooled Bo Gu and Zhou En-lai. Some 72,000 Red soldiers and 15,000 other communists slipped through Chiang's encirclement and set out for Shaanxi province in northern China. Their exhausting

Chiang Kai-shek (standing), Chinese general and politician, poses in 1923 with Sun Yat-sen, leader of the Chinese Nationalist Party (Guomindang) and founding father and first provisional president of the Republic of China.

trek of about 6,000 miles (9,700 kilometers) became known as the Long March.

Mao Zedong was among the fleeing communists. An official account reported that he was "wearing a grey cloth uniform and military cap, carrying two blankets, a cotton sheet, an oilcloth, a coat, a broken umbrella and a bundle of books, abandoning his two-year-old son, whom he would never see again as he set out on a decisive lap of his ascent to power."[1] The marchers crossed barren plateaus, foul swamplands, 24 major rivers (including the Dadu), and 18 mountain ranges. Only about 6,000 survived the march. Along the long route to Shaanxi, Mao ascended to the leadership of the Chinese Communist Party.

In the meantime, the Japanese had invaded Manchuria and turned it into a puppet state named Manchukuo. They further extended their influence into Inner Mongolia and other parts of northern China. Chiang yielded to a number of Japanese demands. His failure to resist the Japanese aggressors angered many students and academics. But Chiang felt ill-prepared to fight the

Mao Zedong (left), Chinese communist revolutionary and founder of the People's Republic of China, is shown in this 1935 photo with fellow revolutionary Zhou En-lai, who would become its first premier.

In 1936, Manchurian forces kidnapped Chiang Kai-shek. They released him only after he agreed to end the civil war and form a united front against the Japanese.

Japanese and the communists at the same time. His first priority was to defeat the communists.

On July 7, 1937, an armed incident at the Marco Polo Bridge outside Beijing touched off the Second Sino-Japanese War (1937–45). Japanese soldiers on a training exercise fired on a Chinese garrison. Chinese soldiers returned fire, and the war was on. The Japanese called it the "China Incident." To the Chinese, it began what came to be known as the "War of Resistance." Japanese armies quickly overcame Chinese resistance. By the end of 1938, the Japanese controlled most of eastern China.

Chiang withdrew his Nationalist forces to Sichuan province and established his wartime capital in Chongqing. Communists—now based in Yan'an in Shaanxi province—joined with Nationalists to form the Second United Front against the Japanese. The fighting continued and merged with World War II.

For the Chinese communists, the war provided a chance for political and military expansion. They reoccupied large areas in northern China that Japanese forces had taken but lacked the troop strength to defend. Drawing on the local peasantry, they enlarged their army and trained the people to become productive Party members. By redistributing land to the peasants in communist-controlled areas, they started a social revolution in the countryside.

While living in a wealthy merchant's house in Yan'an, Mao Zedong used his time to sharpen his grasp of communist doctrine. "If Mao was to become the accepted leader of his Party," observed author Jonathan Spence, "he not only had to win on the battlefield and have successful policies for rural and urban revolution, he also had to be able to hold his own as a theorist."[2]

Smoke billows from a Chinese city following heavy bombardment from Japanese forces during the fighting between the two sides in the late 1930s.

During this period, Mao wrote two essays that would later become military classics. "Problems of Strategy in Guerrilla War" dealt with the many military principles he had developed during his Jiangxi days. His strategies involved "chess-like" moves and countermoves played out against a larger enemy across China's vast checkerboard countryside. In "On Protracted War," he tried to prepare his followers for the long and difficult war that such a strategy would require. "Weapons are an important factor in war," Mao wrote, "but not the decisive factor; it is people, not things, that are decisive."[3]

World War II finally ended in 1945. China emerged victorious but war-torn and economically challenged. The cost in Chinese civilian lives may have been as high as 20 million. And the continued distrust between the communists and the Nationalists did not promise much hope for a lasting peace in China.

The United States tried to avert a military confrontation between the communists and the Nationalists, but to no avail. Both factions wanted complete control over China; both sides were determined to settle for nothing less. Despite the sizeable gains in troop strength made by the communists during the war years, Chiang's armies were still three times larger—and better equipped—than Mao's forces. Yet Mao appeared undaunted by the apparent disadvantage. He considered Chiang and his armies a "paper tiger."

"We have only millet [grain] plus rifles to rely on," Mao wrote, "but history will finally prove that our millet plus rifles is more powerful than Chiang Kai-shek's aeroplanes plus tanks. . . . The reason is simply this: the reactionaries represent reaction, we represent progress."[4] Armed with this certainty of cause, Mao's Red Army—renamed as the People's Liberation Army (PLA)—clashed with Chiang's forces in the spring of 1946. The Chinese Civil War resumed in earnest.

Mao launched a concerted campaign to drive GMD forces out of Manchuria. He called the resumption of fighting the "War of Liberation." By the last half of 1947, volunteers and GMD defectors had doubled the size of the PLA to two million troops. Mao imparted his long experience to his soldiers: "Be sure to fight no battle unprepared," he urged. "Fight no battle you are not sure of winning."[5] His simple maxims paid off.

At the end of World War II in August 1945, the communists held an area with a population of about 100 million.

By November 1948, the PLA had conquered Manchuria. Then it rolled on to capture the vital railhead at Xuzhou in December and topple the port city of Tianjin and the old capital of Beijing a month later. Nanjing, Chiang's capital on the southern banks of the Yangtze River, fell to the PLA in April. Shanghai surrendered in May, followed by Changsha in August.

After World War II, fighting resumed between Mao Zedong's communist forces and Chiang Kai-shek's Nationalist armies. Communist soldiers are shown here escorting Nationalist prisoners in May 1946.

The PLA crossed the Yangtze and continued to drive GMD forces into southern China and off the mainland. Before the year was out, Chiang would withdraw to the offshore islands of Taiwan and Hainan. With millet and rifles—and superior military tactics—Mao had defeated Chiang's "aeroplanes and tanks" in the fight for China's future.

On September 30, 1949, the Central Committee of the Communist Party named Mao Zedong as chairman of the People's Republic of China. The next day, Mao stood on the Gate of Heavenly Peace, overlooking Tiananmen Square in Beijing, and formally announced the founding of the new communist Chinese state. China's future was firmly in communist hands.

Chinese leader Mao Zedong reads the Proclamation of the Central People's Government. The reading took place as part of the founding ceremony of the People's Republic of China in Beijing on October 1, 1949.

BUTLER MIDDLE SCHOOL
310 NORTH HINE AVENUE
WAUKESHA, WI 53188

CHAPTER 4
An Emerging China

The creation of the People's Republic of China (PRC) ushered in a new era in China's long history. Mao Zedong warned the Party that it faced new and uncertain dangers as it headed into uncharted territory. "The achievement of nationwide victory is only the first step in a Long March," he said. "The Chinese Revolution is a great revolution, but the road beyond is longer and the work to come greater and more arduous . . . We should be capable of not only destroying the old world. We must also be capable of creating the new."[1] Chairman Mao and his lieutenants set right to work. First they firmly established their hold on the country, then tackled the enormous task of rebuilding it.

As Party chairman, Mao oversaw every aspect of China's recovery from the devastation of 12 years of war. Zhou En-lai, now the premier, directed all government departments and ministries. Liu Shaoqi, another veteran of the Long March, concentrated on domestic affairs.

Mao Zedong (far right) joins a gathering of Soviet officials in celebration of Soviet dictator Joseph Stalin's 70th birthday. Stalin stands to Mao's immediate right. Sino-Soviet relations broke down in the late 1950s.

Mao reluctantly appealed to the Soviet Union for military, technical, and economic aid. He did not enjoy having to ask Soviet leader Joseph Stalin for help. But with the widening Cold War rift between the Soviet Union and the United States, Mao had nowhere else to turn. He told Stalin that China needed "three to five years of peace" to "bring the country back to pre-war levels, and stabilize the country in general."[2] Mao's efforts yielded a $300 million loan and the Sino-Soviet Treaty of Friendship.

In 1950, the People's Liberation Army seized Hainan from the Republic of China, occupied Tibet, and defeated nearly all of Chiang's remaining forces in Yunnan and Xinjiang Provinces. But that same year, the last thing Mao needed happened. North Korea

Liu Shaoqi (1898–1969), Chinese revolutionary, theorist, and statesman, served as the second chairman of the People's Republic of China. He was considered Mao's successor until being purged in the late 1960s.

invaded South Korea on June 25. After initial battlefield successes, the North Koreans were pushed back deep into their own territory.

In October 1950, with forces of the United Nations (UN) under the leadership of the United States nearing North Korea's border with China on the Yalu River, Mao decided to enter the Korean War. Fearing that the United States was trying to undermine his new government, he sent 300,000 People's Volunteers across the Yalu into North Korea. The war seesawed back and forth and settled into a stalemate that ended in a cease-fire in July 1953. Fighting the United States to a standstill lent prestige to China's new communist regime. But the conflict cost an estimated $2.5 billion and nearly 400,000 casualties, according to official Chinese sources.

In 1953, Mao introduced a Five-Year Economic Plan to stimulate industrial development. At the same time, the PRC government seized landholdings from landlords and redistributed them among the peasants. Mobs of mistreated farmers retaliated against landlords everywhere. As many as a million were executed.

> Chairman Mao encouraged population growth. Under his leadership, China's population almost doubled, from about 550 million to more than 900 million.

Over the five-year span, China's industry grew at the rapid rate of 15 percent a year. But agriculture lagged behind. Some peasants were persuaded to combine their landholdings into farming cooperatives. Others had to be forced to do that. Agricultural output improved, but at a slower rate than industry. By 1957, the communists had harnessed all principal industries under government reins.

The following year, Mao embarked on a second Five-Year Plan to exploit his country's greatest resource — its vast population. He called his vision the Great Leap Forward. Mao intended to speed development by using more laborers and having them work longer hours. His plan called for setting up many small factories and combining small cooperatives into huge communes for better efficiency. Mao's idea failed to take China's lack of capital and technology into account. His forward leap sent China's economy teetering backward.

From 1959 to 1961, China suffered economic depression, food shortages, and a decline in industrial production. Its agricultural system was disrupted. And a series of natural disasters resulted in the deaths of up to 20 million people from starvation. The Soviets' withdrawal of technical support added to the calamity. As a result, friendly relations between China and the Soviet Union broke down.

"The Great Leap had ended in an apocalyptic failure," observes author Philip Short. "His [Mao's] grandiose dream of universal plenty had been metamorphosed into an epic of pure horror."[3] The Leap was officially abandoned in 1960. But Mao had another dream.

A recovering economy stirred disagreement among Party members in 1962. Party "radicals" differed with "revisionists" about how to achieve economic growth while sticking with

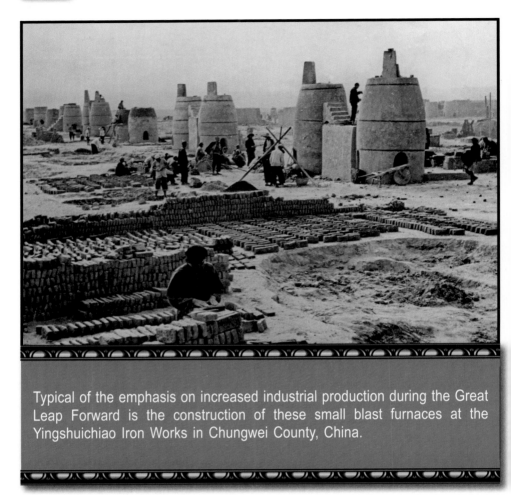

Typical of the emphasis on increased industrial production during the Great Leap Forward is the construction of these small blast furnaces at the Yingshuichiao Iron Works in Chungwei County, China.

communist principles. Radicals wanted a classless society in which everyone worked toward the common good. Revisionists believed economic growth would come only by changing the ruling class of society from the laboring class to the middle class.

In 1966, Mao lent his support to the radical faction. He started a program called the Great Proletarian Cultural Revolution, or simply the Cultural Revolution. It strove to strictly enforce communist doctrine and rid China of revisionists. Radicals purged many top government leaders and officials for failing to follow the Party line. Students and other young people formed paramilitary groups call the Red Guards. They shut down schools

In 1972, US President Richard M. Nixon visited Chairman Mao Zedong in China. They signed the Shanghai Communique, which cleared the way for improved relations between their two countries.

and attacked revisionists, intellectuals, scientists, and all things they considered to be "anti-Mao." A wave of terror washed over the land.

"Chairman Mao called on us to rebel, to bombard, to destroy, and we did so without hesitation," one Shanghai student leader recalled. "Just like a bunch of mad dogs, once angered each tries to be madder than the rest."[4]

The madness of the Cultural Revolution continued until Mao's death in 1976. Zhou En-lai died the same year. Their deaths touched off a power struggle between radicals led by Mao's widow, Jiang Qing, and moderates championed by Deng Xiaoping, an important official who had been purged during the Cultural Revolution. Hua Geofeng surfaced as a compromise choice to replace both Zhou and Mao as premier and chairman. Hua's government imprisoned Jiang and three other radicals called the Gang of Four. They were blamed for the excesses of the Cultural Revolution.

Deng Xiaoping was named vice premier and vice chairman of the Chinese Communist Party. Though Deng never formally became the elected head of state or government, he effectively served as the leader of the People's Republic of China from 1978 to the early 1990s. China adopted its present constitution under Deng's guidance in 1982.

Deng instituted significant economic reforms known as "socialist market economy" or "socialism with Chinese characteristics." He opened China to the global market and vastly improved the Chinese standard of living. Deng is generally credited with developing China into one of the fastest-growing economies in the world. Despite his economic openness, he firmly opposed political reform. He died in 1997.

Deng Xiaoping, deputy premier of the People's Republic of China, is greeted by US President Jimmy Carter at the White House on January 29, 1979. The two men signed historic accords that opened the door to better US-China relations.

China continued to prosper under successive leaders in the 1990s and through the first decade of the twenty-first century. In November 2012, China's Eighteenth National Communist Party Congress replaced Hu Jintao and Wen Jiabao as president and premier with Xi Jinping and Li Keqiang. The new leaders formally took office in 2013.

In describing President Xi Jinping, Chinese publisher Pin Ho writes, "Vocally, he's a nationalist. Psychologically, he greatly hopes to keep good relations with the West, especially the US."[5] The West would welcome good relations from an increasingly powerful China.

Premier Li Keqiang (right) and General Secretary of the Chinese Communist Party Xi Jinping stand during the closing ceremony of the National People's Congress (NPC) in Beijing in March, 2014. With about 3,000 members the NPC is the world's largest legislative body.

CHAPTER 5
China Today

China's new President Xi Jinping faced "the challenges of adapting China to the consequences of its success."[1] In an interview with former US Secretary of State Henry Kissinger, Xi defined his aims as "a sweeping reform program designed to move millions to the cities, streamline bureaucracy, reorient the economy away from state-owned enterprises and fight corruption."[2]

His success requires the cooperation of his people and the support of the Chinese Communist Party (CCP), the ruling party of the People's Republic of China. The CCP exists alongside the United Front, a coalition of governing political parties. In practice, however, the CCP is the *only* party in China. Its legal authority is guaranteed by the National Constitution, and it stands above the law.

The CCP's organizational structure was rebuilt after Mao's Cultural Revolution. Its political ideology no longer follows Marxism, Leninism, and the thoughts of Mao Zedong. Instead, it has returned to the Confucianist doctrine that has influenced

The 18th National Congress of the Communist Party of China concludes its session in the Great Hall of the People in Beijing on November 14, 2012.

Chinese society and shaped its worldview for centuries. Confucianism emphasizes the virtues of humaneness, benevolence, morality, loyalty, and filial piety (children's respect toward their parents). The Party believes these virtues lead to a harmonious society.

In theory, the CCP's highest body is the National Congress, which meets at least once every five years. The CCP's primary organs of power are the Central Committee and the Central Discipline Inspection Commission. The Central Committee includes the General Secretary, the Politburo Standing Committee, and the Central Military Commission.

Xi Jinping is the current party leader (2014). He holds the title of General Secretary of the Central Committee. It is the highest office within the party. Though the Central Committee is often represented as the CCP's leading body, the Politburo and its Standing Committee make the decisions on all major issues.

The politics of China exist within a framework of a single-party socialist republic. Elections are based on a hierarchical system. Local People's Congresses are directly elected by the people. All higher levels of People's Congresses up to the National People's Congress are elected indirectly by the People's Congress of the level immediately below. The National People's Congress is the national legislative body.

The government of the People's Republic of China (PRC) exercises administrative control over 22 provinces. It claims Taiwan as its 23rd province. Taiwan is governed by the Republic of China, which contests the PRC's claim.

The PRC also has five autonomous (self-governing) regions. Notable among them are the disputed region of Tibet and

Despite China's flourishing economy, the disparity between rural and urban areas continues to grow. In 2010, rural residents had an annual income of 5,900 yuan ($898) compared to 19,100 yuan ($2,900) for urban dwellers.

Members of the Tibetan Youth Congress demonstrate against Chinese rule in Tibet to honor Tibetan National Uprising Day in Bangalore, India, on March 10, 2014. Tibetans from all across the globe gathered in India to commemorate the 55th anniversary of Tibetan resistance.

Xinjiang, the home of Muslim Uighurs in the northwest. Two Special Administrative Regions—Hong Kong and Macau—enjoy a high degree of autonomy under the principle of "one country, two systems." The large municipalities of Beijing, Shanghai, Chongqing, and Tianjin share equal political status with the provinces.

In the People's Republic of China, the government is responsible for planning and managing the national economy. According to one US study, however, "the concept of government supervision of the economy had changed . . . from one of direct but stifling state control to one of indirect guidance of a more dynamic economy."[3] Other aspects of life under China's single-party socialist republic are still tightly controlled.

Hong Kong, China

The State keeps a firm hand on traditional media (television, radio, films, books, periodicals, etc.) and new media (internet, email, texting, and so on). It limits access to foreign websites on the internet and uses monitoring systems to control political activism. China's Great Firewall—or Golden Shield—is notorious for blocking such popular social networking sites as Facebook, YouTube, and Twitter. The sale of game consoles has been banned in China since 2000 to safeguard children's mental and physical development.

Since 1979, China has maintained a one-child policy to control its population. It restricts urban couples to only one child. Exceptions are allowed in some cases. They include twins, rural couples, ethnic minorities, and couples who are both only children themselves. Hong and Macau are exempted from this policy, along with foreigners living in China.

A valid passport is required to obtain a Chinese visa. The passport must contain blank visa pages, a passport photo, and a completed visa application. Chinese people are friendly and welcome foreign visitors.

China is officially atheist, but the constitution guarantees freedom of religion. Buddhism and Christianity are growing rapidly in China. Other religions include Taoism, Islam, and various folk religions.

But religious freedom is not entirely free. The State believes that religion breeds disloyalty, separatism, and subversion. It therefore exercises control over religious organizations through a registration process and monitoring all religious activities. In Tibet, in an effort to limit the influence of the Dalai Lama, the CCP has forbidden his reincarnation without permission of the government.

In 1992, a new spiritual discipline called Falun Gong ("Dharma Wheel Practice") was introduced. Since then, human rights watchers have reported that Falun Gong practitioners in China have suffered a wide range of human rights abuses. They estimate hundreds of thousands have been imprisoned and subjected to hard labor. "Tens of millions of Chinese were attracted to the teachings of the Falun Gong," writes Yale professor John Bryan Starr, "despite its having been condemned by the party-state as a 'superstitious cult.'"[4]

Despite government restrictions on freedom of association and speech, protests and dissident movements are on the rise in China. Notable dissents include the 1979 uprising against communist rule in Tibet, and the 1989 Tiananmen Square protest that was put down by the military. Uighur protests in Xinjiang in April 2013 left 21 people dead in what the government described as an act of terror.

Starting with 8,700 "mass group incidents" in 1993, large demonstrations increased to some 180,000 events in 2010. Pro-

Chinese people struggle with their government over land rights. All land is owned by the state; individuals own the physical property on it. Popular dissent over land seizures by corrupt developers and officials poses a growing threat to the government.

democracy protests inspired by, and named after, the Jasmine Revolution in Tunisia broke out in several cities in February 2011. Police arrested 35 dissidents and about 25 journalists.

In China's criminal justice system, police have the power to hold people at unknown locations for up to six months. The age for bearing criminal responsibility is 16. Chinese law provides four categories of punishments: control (monitoring), criminal detention, fixed term imprisonment, and life imprisonment and death.

As a superpower, the People's Republic of China maintains diplomatic relations with 171 countries. Today's China has moved from imperial rule, through republican and communist rule, to arrive at its present status as a single-party socialist republic. It still faces formidable problems, such as population growth, human rights, Taiwan and Tibet issues, environmental concerns, a new arms race, cybersecurity, currency manipulation and piracy in global trade, and more.

President Xi Jinping stands at the helm of China's ship of state. He must hold fast to his station, while charting a true course through the treacherous waters of unsolved problems. The world wishes him smooth sailing.

Following a press conference in the Great Hall of the People in Beijing in November 2009, US President Barack Obama (left) and Chinese President Hu Jintao shake hands in a gesture of mutual goodwill.

TIMELINE

221–206 BCE   Qin dynasty establishes the first great Chinese empire.

1636 CE   Manchus found the Qing dynasty.

1861   Qing Emperor Xianfeng dies; his six-year-old son Tongzhi succeeds him but Dowager Empress Cixi wields real power behind the throne.

1875   Qing Emperor Tongzhi dies; three-year-old Guangxu succeeds him as Cixi retains power.

1900   Boxers rebel against foreigners in China.

1908   Qing Emperor Guangxu dies on November 14; two-year-old Puyi succeeds him.

1911   Xinhai Revolution erupts.

1912   Xinhai Revolution ends with the founding of the Republic of China; Yuan Shikai is elected president on March 10.

1916   Yuan Shikai abdicates on March 21.

1921   Chinese Communist Party (CCP) is founded in Shanghai.

1926–27   Chiang Kai-shek leads the Northern Expedition against Chinese warlords.

1927   Chinese Civil War erupts between the forces of the Nationalist Party and the Chinese Communist Party.

1928   Chiang Kai-shek is named Generalissimo of all Chinese forces. Mao Zedong and Zhu De merge their forces to form the Fourth Red Army.

1930–34   Chiang Kai-shek conducts five Encirclement Campaigns against the communists in southern China.

1934–35   Mao Zedong leads the Long March from Jiangxi Province to Shaanxi Province.

1936   Manchurian forces kidnap and release Chiang Kai-shek.

1937   An armed incident at the Marco Polo Bridge touches off the Sino-Japanese War; the war merges with World War II and ends in August 1945.

1946   Chinese Civil War resumes.

1949   Communists defeat Nationalists. Mao Zedong is named Chairman of the People's Republic of China on September 30 and announces the founding of the new Communist Chinese state the next day.

1950   North Korea invades South Korea; the war rages for three years.

1953   Mao Zedong introduces Five-Year Economic plan.

1958   Mao embarks on a second Five-Year Economic plan called the Great Leap Forward.

1966   Mao starts a program called the Great Proletarian Cultural Revolution.

1972   US President Richard M. Nixon visits Mao Zedong in China.

1976   Mao Zedong dies on September 9.

1978   Deng Xiaoping effectively serves as the leader of the People's Republic of China until the early 1990s.

1989   Chinese soldiers open fire on protestors in Tiananmen Square, killing hundreds.

1997   Deng Xiaoping dies on February 19.

TIMELINE

2012   China's Eighteenth National Communist Party Congress replaces Hu Jintao and Wen Jiabao as president and premier with Xi Jinping and Li Keqiang.

2013   Xi Jinping and Li Keqiang take office on March 17.

2014   Chinese government suppresses any observations of 25th anniversary of Tiananmen Square massacre.

CHAPTER NOTES

Chapter 1. Looking Back to See the Future

1. Philip Short, *Mao: A Life* (New York: Henry Holt and Company, 1999), p. 326.

2. Jonathan Fenby, *Modern China: The Fall and Rise of a Great Power, 1850 to the Present* (New York: HarperCollins Publishers, 2008), p. 258.

3. "Confucius: Confucianism" http://www.spaceandmotion.com/ Philosophy-Confucius-Confucianism.htm

4. Fenby, p. 5.

Chapter 2. Two Leaders Emerge

1. Bertil Lintner, *Blood Brothers: The Criminal Underworld of Asia* (New York: Palgrave Macmillan, 2002), p. 51.

2. Philip Short, *Mao: A Life* (New York: Henry Holt and Company, 1999), p. 40.

3. Jonathan Fenby, *Modern China: The Fall and Rise of a Great Power, 1850 to the Present* (New York: HarperCollins Publishers, 2008), p. 127.

4. Short, p. 82.

5. Jonathan Spence, *Mao Zedong.* Penguin Lives Series. (New York: Viking, 1999), p. 75.

Chapter 3. Fighting for China' s Future

1. Jonathan Fenby, *Modern China: The Fall and Rise of a Great Power, 1850 to the Present* (New York: HarperCollins Publishers, 2008), p. 251.

2. Jonathan Spence, *Mao Zedong.* Penguin Lives Series. (New York: Viking, 1999), p. 94.

3. Philip Short, *Mao: A Life* (New York: Henry Holt and Company, 1999), p. 364.

4. Ibid., p. 414.

5. Spence, p. 107.

Chapter 4. An Emerging China

1. Philip Short, *Mao: A Life* (New York: Henry Holt and Company, 1999), p. 418.

2. Jonathan Spence, *Mao Zedong.* Penguin Lives Series. (New York: Viking, 1999), p. 110.

3. Short, p. 505.

4. Jonathan Fenby, *Modern China: The Fall and Rise of a Great Power, 1850 to the Present* (New York: HarperCollins Publishers, 2008), p. 456.

5. Elizabeth Yuan, "Xi Jinping: 'Princeling' to China's president." CNN, March 14, 2013. http://www.cnn.com/2013/03/04/ world/asia/xi-jinping-profile

Chapter 5. China Today

1. Henry Kissinger, "Xi Jinping: President of China, 59," The 2013 TIME 100. *Time*, April 18, 2013. http://time100.time.com/2013/04/ 18/time-100/slide/xi-jinping/

2. Ibid.

3. Robert L. Worden, Andrea Matles Savada, and Ronald E. Dolan (editors). "Roles of the Government and Party," in *China: A Country Study.* Washington, DC: GPO for the Library of Congress, 1987. http://countrystudies.us.china/ 93.htm

4. John Bryan Starr, *Understanding China: A Guide to China's Economy, History, and Political Culture.* 3rd ed. (New York: Hill and Wang, 2010), p. 158.

FURTHER READING

Books for Children and Young Adults

Block, Marta Segal. *Modern China*. China Focus Series. North Mankato, MN: Heinemann, 2009.

Malaspina, Ann. *The Chinese Revolution and Mao Zedong in World History*. In World History Series. Berkeley Heights, NJ: Enslow Publishers, 2004.

Slavicek, Louise Chipley. *Mao Zedong*. Great Military Leaders of the 20th Century Series. New York: Chelsea House/Infobase, 2004.

Streissguth, Tom. *China in the 21st Century: A New World Power*. Issues in Focus Today Series. Berkeley Heights, NJ: Enslow Publishers, 2008.

Uschan, Michael V. *China Since World War II*. World History Series. Farmington Hills, MI: Lucent Books, 2008.

Works Consulted
Books

Fairbank, John King, and Merle Goldman. *China: A New History*. 2d enlarged ed. Cambridge, MA: The Belknap Press of Harvard University Press, 2006.

Fenby, Jonathan. *Modern China: The Fall and Rise of a Great Power, 1850 to the Present*. New York: HarperCollins Publishers, 2008.

Hahn, Emily. *China to Me*. Boston: Beacon Press, 1994.

Kristof, Nicholas D., and Sheryl WuDunn. *China Wakes: The Struggle for the Soul of a Rising Power*. New York: Vintage Books, 1994.

Lintner, Bertil. *Blood Brothers: The Criminal Underworld of Asia*. New York: Palgrave Macmillan, 2002.

Mao Tse-tung. *On Guerrilla Warfare*. Translated by Samuel B. Griffith. New York: Praeger Publishers, 1961.

Mitter, Rana. *Modern China*. New York: Sterling Publishing, 2009.

FURTHER READING

Pan, Philip P. *Out of Mao's Shadow: The Struggle for the Soul of a New China*. New York: Simon & Schuster Paperbacks, 2009.

Short, Philip. *Mao: A Life*. New York: Henry Holt and Company, 1999.

Spence, Jonathan. *Mao Zedong*. Penguin Lives Series. New York: Viking, 1999.

Starr, John Bryan. *Understanding China: A Guide to China's Economy, History, and Political Culture*. 3rd ed. New York: Hill and Wang, 2010.

Taylor, Robert H., ed. *Asia and the Pacific*. Vol. 1. Handbooks to the Modern World. New York: Facts on File/Infobase, 1991.

On the Internet
Confucius: Confucianism
   http://www.spaceandmotion.com/Philosophy-Confucius-Confucianism.htm

Kissinger, Henry. "Xi Jinping: President of China, 59," The 2013 TIME 100. *Time*, April 18, 2013. http://time100.time.com/2013/04/18/time-100/slide/xi-jinping/

Worden, Robert L., Andrea Matles Savada, and Ronald E. Dolan (editors). "Roles of the Government and Party," in *China: A Country Study*. Washington, DC: GPO for the Library of Congress, 1987. http://countrystudies.us.china/93.htm

Yuan, Elizabeth. "Xi Jinping: 'Princeling' to China's president." CNN, March 4, 2013. http://www.cnn.com/2013/03/04/world/asia/xi-jinping-profile

PHOTO CREDITS: All design elements from Thinkstock/Sharon Beck; Cover—pp. 5, 8, 9, 10, 11, 13, 38—Thinkstock; pp. 7, 19, 27—akg-images/Newscom; p. 14—Library of Congress, LC-DIG-jpd-02533; p. 16—Hulton Archive/Getty Images; p. 20—Keystone/Getty Images; p. 22—Popperfoto/Getty Images; p. 24—George Lacks/Time & Life Pictures/Getty Images; p. 25—Xinhua/ZUMAPRESS/Newscom; p. 28—KEYSTONE Pictures USA/ZUMAPRESS/Newscom; p. 30—Sovfoto/UIG via Getty Images; p. 31—National Archives, 194759; p. 32—National Archives, 183157; p. 33—ADRIAN BRADSHAW/EPA/Newscom; p. 35—Kyodo/Newscom; p. 37—Dreamstime/Midhun Menon; p. 40—White House Photo by Pete Souza; p. 41—CIA.gov.

GLOSSARY

bureaucrat (BYOOR-oh-krat) — An official who works in a government office, especially one who applies the rules of his department without exercising much judgment.

communism (KOM-yu-niz-em) — A social system in which property is owned by the community and each member works for the common benefit.

dowager (DOW-uh-jer) — A woman who holds a title or property from her dead husband.

dynasty (DIE-nuh-stee) — A line of hereditary rulers.

hereditary (huh-RED-ih-tehr-ee) — Inherited; able to be passed or received from one generation to another.

millet (MIL-uht) — A kind of cereal plant growing four to five feet high and producing a large crop of small seeds.

monarchy (MAHN-ahr-kee) — A form of government in which a monarch — a king, queen, emperor, or empress — is the supreme ruler.

provisional (proh-VIZH-uh-nahl) — Arranged or agreed upon temporarily but possibly to be altered later.

reparation (rep-uh-RAY-shon) — Compensation for war damages, demanded by the victor from a defeated enemy.

turbulence (TUR-byu-lence) — A state of commotion or unrest; unruliness.

venerate (VEN-uh-rayt) — To regard with deep respect; to honor as hallowed or sacred.

INDEX

About the Author

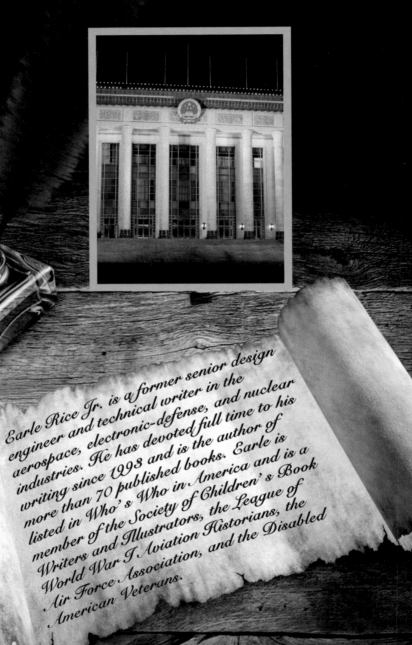

Earle Rice Jr. is a former senior design engineer and technical writer in the aerospace, electronic-defense, and nuclear industries. He has devoted full time to his writing since 1993 and is the author of more than 70 published books. Earle is listed in Who's Who in America and is a member of the Society of Children's Book Writers and Illustrators, the League of World War I Aviation Historians, the Air Force Association, and the Disabled American Veterans.

S0-AEA-177

My Science Library

What's the Weather Like Today?

by Conrad J. Storad

Science Content Editor:
Kristi Lew

Rourke
Educational Media

rourkeeducationalmedia.com

Science content editor: Kristi Lew

A former high school teacher with a background in biochemistry and more than 10 years of experience in cytogenetic laboratories, Kristi Lew specializes in taking complex scientific information and making it fun and interesting for scientists and non-scientists alike. She is the author of more than 20 science books for children and teachers.

© 2012 Rourke Educational Media

All rights reserved. No part of this book may be reproduced or utilized in any form or by any means, electronic or mechanical including photocopying, recording, or by any information storage and retrieval system without permission in writing from the publisher.

www.rourkeeducationalmedia.com

To Eli, Natalie, and Logan. Never stop learning!
-- Grandpa Top

Photo credits:Cover © Rennaulka, Iafoto; Cover logo frog © Eric Pohl, test tube © Sergey Lazarev; Page 5 © SVLuma; Page 6 © alsamua; Page 7 © Ovsyannikova Ekaterina; Page 9 © Ilin Sergey; Page 10 © Pigprox; Page 11 © magaliB;; Page 12 © Bill Frische; Page 13 © Anettphoto; Page 14 © Steve Collender; Page 15 © Dainis Derics; Page 16 © Delmas Lehman; Page 17 © Iafoto; Page 18 © Vladislav Gurfinkel; Page 19 © Ramon Berk; Page 21 © Maxim Petrichuk

Editor: Kelli Hicks

Cover and page design by Nicola Stratford, bdpublishing.com

Library of Congress Cataloging-in-Publication Data

Storad, Conrad J.
 What's the weather like today? / Conrad J. Storad.
     p. cm. -- (My science library)
 Includes bibliographical references and index.
 ISBN 978-1-61741-737-5 (Hard cover) (alk. paper)
 ISBN 978-1-61741-939-3 (Soft cover)
 1. Weather--Juvenile literature. I. Title.
 QC981.3.S76 2012
 551.6--dc22
                          2011003903

Printed in China, FOFO I - Production Company
  Shenzhen, Guangdong Province

Rourke
Educational Media

rourkeeducationalmedia.com

customerservice@rourkeeducationalmedia.com • PO Box 643328 Vero Beach, Florida 32964

Table of Contents

What Is Weather?

Weather happens every day. It is the condition of the sky above and the outside air all around us.

The weather affects what we do each day. Is today a good day to play outside?

Weather can change by the hour or by the day. It can also stay the same for many days or weeks.

Blue skies can quickly turn stormy.

Snow can collect in deep piles during the winter.

How Weather Works

Weather isn't just one thing. Air, heat, water, and **energy** work together to make our weather each day.

Hot air rises. It carries tiny drops of water high into the sky. The drops form into **clouds**.

Cirrus clouds usually mean it's a good day to play outside.

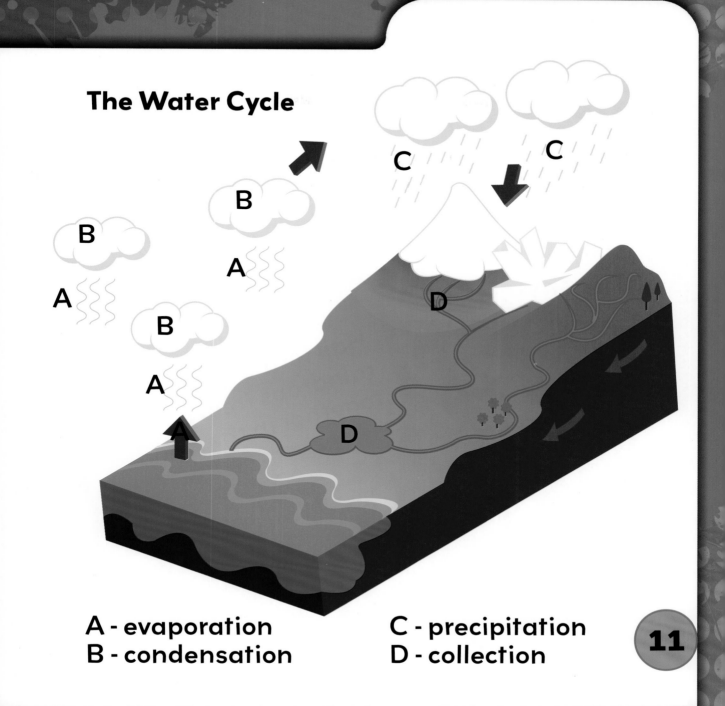

The Water Cycle

A - evaporation
B - condensation
C - precipitation
D - collection

11

Stormy Weather

Thunder and **lightning** can happen during stormy weather. Rain, hail, or snow may fall from the sky.

Hail forms when many raindrops freeze together in the clouds.

Lightning is a flash of electricity produced by a thunderstorm.

13

Snowflakes form in clouds when water droplets freeze. A blizzard is a storm with lots of snow.

Look at these snowflakes. No two are exactly alike.

A **tornado** is a violent windstorm. It looks like a dark cloud shaped like a funnel.

A tornado is also called a twister. It can smash buildings to pieces.

17

A **hurricane** is one of the biggest storms of all. Hurricanes are made of powerful wind and lots of rain.

the eye

Hurricane winds spin around a center point called the eye.

Hurricane winds can blow from 74 to over 155 miles (119-249 kilometers) per hour.

19

Sometimes a **rainbow** appears when a storm is almost over. Sunlight shines through water drops to form a rainbow.

21

SHOW What You Know

1. Is weather the same all the time, or does it change?

2. Besides rain, what else can fall from the clouds?

3. Name some types of stormy weather.

Glossary

clouds (KLOUDZ): visible masses of tiny water drops or ice particles suspended in the air

energy (EN-ur-gee): the ability of something to do work or a source of power

hurricane (HUR-I-kane): a violent storm with heavy rain and high winds

lightning (LITE-ning): a flash of light in the sky when electricity moves between clouds or between a cloud and the ground

rainbow (RAYN-boh): an arch of different colors caused by the bending of sunlight as it shines through water vapor

thunder (THUHN-der): the loud sound during a storm that comes after a flash of lightning

tornado (tor-NAY-doh): a violent and very destructive windstorm that appears as a dark cloud shaped like a funnel

weather (WETH-ur): the condition of the outside air or atmosphere at a particular time and place

Index

Websites

www.theweatherchannelkids.com/

www.wxdude.com/kidres.html

www.Illiniweather.com

www.tornadochaser.com

About the Author

Conrad J. Storad is the award-winning author of more than 30 books for young readers. He writes about desert animals, plants, creepy crawlers, and planets. Conrad lives in Tempe, Arizona with his wife Laurie, and their little double dapple wiener dog, Sophia. They love to explore Arizona's deserts and mountains.

Photo by Tom Story